AMERICA IS ONE SICK MF: Why Greed-Driven America Went Off The Rails....

By

Jim Green

DEDICATED TO:

Those dedicated to fixing it….

ISBN-13: 978-1479378654

ISBN-10: 1479378658

PROLOGUE

America is one sick MF—

We have elements in America that will say that I "hate" America for making that statement—but they would be dead-wrong—

Indeed, it is their ignorance of America--that has America so FU—We cannot start fixing what is wrong with America, until we start fessing-up to what we are doing wrong— And when we cannot tell the truth in a "free" country—it is no longer a "free" country….Further, the following are "institutional flaws" that call for the

American people to step up—and getting rid of the current crop of Republicans: governors, in our state houses, and in Washington, would be a good start....

In the governor race in Texas in 1994, Governor Ann Richards remarked in response to a concern for the explosion of prison building in Texas at the time "If you violate the law in Texas, we have a place to lock you up."

The remark didn't help Governor Richards to get re-elected [she lost to W]—and in spite of her prison reforms—the statement was to appease an electorate [suffering from intense feelings of low self-esteem—more on the political implications of this epidemic later] that had taken a sharp turn to the right—

and straight into bananaville—[which has metastasized—and gotten even more widespread and rigid in the years since—and includes a racism vote in this election].

For instance, we are six weeks out from the 2012 election [we will probably know the result by the time this is published]—but given the destructive, almost fatal damage done to America when W was appointed to the presidency—this election should not even be close and President Obama should win it hands down [at least by 20 points-- and he may yet] but as I write it is neck-and-neck—Impossible if we had an informed and rational electorate—and suffering from severe amnesia!

So where is the evidence that "America is one sick MF"? Consider this:

We have the same prison population as China—but they have a billion more people! No other civilized country in the world even comes close to our incarceration rate—and our PR is that we are the most free? We have 5% of the world's population, and 25% of all prison inmates on earth—in our prisons! And since 1990 it has also in many states become a privatized "for profit" criminal industry!

Further, 70% of our prison population are in for "non-violent" offenses, and we daily turn non-violent offenders into violent career criminals—even disregarding the destruction to our family units--by our insane incarceration rate!

We pay twice as much for healthcare in America, for half the result [only a slight exaggeration]—than any other industrial country in the world—and this is for only one reason: PURE GREED!

We have a tiny handful of "profiteers"—who don't even so much as put a Band-Aid on a patient—who annually siphon billions of dollars out of our healthcare system for their own personal aggrandizement and GREEDY self-interests—leaving 44,000 American to die every year due to the high costs of healthcare—and their GREED has relegated America to 37th in the world in healthcare, according to the World Health Organization!

And GREED is so pervasive in our healthcare system that it has become a magnet for persons who see it as a way to get rich, rather than the time-honored goal of medicine—to cure the ill.

And when we look at our gun violence in America, we need to ask: Why do we have this unconscionable gun violence? The sheer numbers of homicides by handguns, alone, tells the whole story: Canada 151, Australia 57, Germany 373, Japan 19, England and Wales 54, the United States 11,789 [numbers which remain relatively static year after year]! And, when we add in all deaths by guns, including the fact that 9 children are killed by guns everyday in America, our gun violence escalates to a staggering 28,663!

As one astute observer noted, "The drug war is over—we lost"—and while we claim that by criminalizing drugs we are keeping them out of the hands of our youth, but as every middle school student knows—it is 10 times easier to get pot, than alcohol, because it is regulated by the state.

Further, half of the persons we have in our prisons are in for drug-related offenses [either directly or indirectly]—

Our war on drugs is a "lose-lose-lose proposition: the loss of tens of billions to maintain our prisons, the loss of dollars to educate our youth [which are competing for the same tax dollars], and the loss in tax revenue by our not decriminalizing drugs—even disregarding the health and hemp benefits of pot!

But the mother of all shortcomings in America, is our unemployment crisis—which existed before Bush II made it infinitely worse—but persists because we still have one foot on the plantation—and insist that it is only the "market" that can create jobs!

Unemployment is a "social" problem—and the last place we should look to solve this problem is anything as unstable and erratic as the "market", which only hires people to increase their "profit", not to solve "social" problems—I am a capitalist---I want the market to succeed—but the objectives are distinctly different….and at present we undermine the Market—in the erroneous belief of helping it—more on this below--

For clarity, we should never condemn the CEO who closes a plant because they are losing money, but we should be outraged by a government that is indifferent or inept in addressing the "social" problems caused by this lapse in the market.

This does not mean that the government should create jobs—[frequently misperceived as WPA] but rather, create and enforce laws that will fill this void within the framework of 15 USC § 3101—which "authorizes" the creation of a "reservoir of public employment" at any time our unemployment in America exceeds "3%" [a Pro-Market solution].

For instance, HR 870 currently pending in the House, or the proposed Neighbor-To-Neighbor Job Creation Act: A federally mandated, mutual insurance—owned by our employed to provide a fund to hire/train our unemployed. See also: www.Inclusivism.org

For a modest policy cost of 4% of salary we can reduce our unemployment to 3%, within one year of passage—and this solution will create more "private sector" jobs in 6 months, than our current legislation [HR 2847, the HIRE Act] in 6 years, if ever! See more detail: MY LETTERS TO PRESIDENT

OBAMA, and OUR GREED AND IGNORANCE, on Amazon/Kindle.

IN SUM, regarding all of the above: The world has changed, our solutions haven't, and the result has been a disaster—and many of our current solutions could be compared to pouring gasoline on a fire, to put it out—

A MAJOR step forward in addressing many of the problems, above [including prison reform]—is for "Conventional Wisdom" to reverse our job creation formula—

At present, the formula is to fix the market, and the market will then fix our unemployment crisis, i.e., fixing unemployment is a step-child in the formula [this may have worked in the past, but not now or going forward—more on this shortly]—at present we need to reverse field—and fix unemployment and this will, in turn, fix the market.

By following the former--our unemployment needle has barely ticked downward—and the result has been a disaster, socially, economically, and politically--it will take years to get back to "5%"—far outstripping unemployment benefits—and under that formula—if the market fails, the unemployed are out of luck!

In political terms, if the Obama administration had followed the latter: The Tea Party would be meeting in a phone booth--all of their progress would have been bullet-proof—rather than as it has turned out—a target.

The following chapters are self-explanatory [letters to the editor and other papers]—and offer suggestions about how we got where we are, and outline proposed solutions for the above. As Oscar Wilde averred "The only truly worthless opinion is an unbiased one"—so bias, agreed—but always in the interest in getting at the larger goal—the truth….

The above is the "How" we went off the rails—the "Why" is more illusive—here is my take. We are a "representative" government--we hire politicians to "represent" what is in our best economic interests—

But when we have a block of voters [identified above] who are mumbling to themselves about gays getting married, or whether women should be forced to have children [even if they have been raped]— and vote against the economic interests of their own children by voting Republican-- the national Republican Party is then free to pander to the GREED of their wealthiest contributors—AND THIS IS THE SINGULAR GOAL OF THE REPUBLICAN PARTY! They stand for NOTHING else! And all of the solutions, above, are to pander to the interests of the 1%, and at the expense of the 99%!

This phenomenon is the subject of the book "What's The Matter With Kansas?" and asks the question—in a "representative" government—why on earth would anyone in their right mind vote for a politician who doesn't "represent" them [and please don't say only an idiot]?

In short, If one is not a billionaire, and is voting Republican—they need to have their head examined!
This is not about ideology, folks—it is about logic….

Also, this does not need explanation to the two other people who read this book—[and hopefully understands nuance]--but, I love America, otherwise I would not have written the book—and we have some phenomenal accomplishments—We played a major role in defeating Hitler in WW II, we put a man on the Moon, the list goes on and on—but if I had an uncle, that I loved, who went off the rails—and concludes he was born on Krypton, and thought he could fly—and had taken up residence on the neighbor's roof—it would be remiss to look the other way....

Incidentally, I published my first book on my 78th birthday—and have published a book a month since--this is my seventh [and my last]—and not that I write that fast, or well—the materials were all there for the better part of the past 30 years, give or take, gathering dust—it was just a matter of pulling them together in some order—also, don't believe any book should be over 60 pages, plus/minus—i.e., can be read in the crapper--two hours, max--lol]—but it seems best summed up by a very astute observer [wish I could recall their name to give credit] but re the long delay in publishing: Persons who write do so because they have no choice—they become an "author", however, when people start reading what they have written….

Finally, a note to the reader—the papers and letters are not in sequence, and there is some redundancy [please look for the nuggets…Thx--lol]—also, if you are a "typo-wonk"—are more concerned with sentence structure, etc., than content—you probably won't like my writing—and a wayward capital letter, here and there, and appearing out of place and used for emphasis—editorial license—so apologies, here—

Just look for content, please....THX

CHAPTER ONE

THE HISTORY OF HOW WE GOT WHERE
WE ARE:

In the mid-1970's, the colliding forces of
automation, technology, globalization, etc.,
reached a critical mass, resulting in
ubiquitous unemployment in all of the OECD
countries, and has left their leaders
conflicted, ever since, regarding the
displaced employee—Eurozone
unemployment is still in double digits, with
Spain at 22.9%, and with high youth
unemployment a major factor in Arab
Spring.

In the U.S., we took a pro-active role in
addressing, and as a direct response to this

economic shift—and in 1978 President Carter signed into law 15 USC § 3101-- which "authorizes" the creation of a "reservoir of public employment" at any time our unemployment in America exceeds "3%".

The following year, in 1979, however, and in a panic over Humphrey-Hawkins—our ultra-conservative foundations, and desperate to preserve the "market only" job creation concept, embraced a flawed paper by an obscure MIT student, David L. Birch "The Job Generation Process"; and [with lots of cash] gave his paper biblical importance, and every president since has cited his finding as gospel.

Birch's paper concluded that "small businesses" were the greatest generator of new jobs—problem is, for the purposes of policy-making—it is BS. In a study at Harvard University in 2010, "The Myth of Small Business Job Creation" The research shows "no systematic relationship between firm size and growth." And that small businesses can actually detract from job growth—nevertheless, it is still the Republican One and Only job creation solution!

And in spite of this Washington struggles, still, to make this antiquated and unworkable notion, work--that it is only the market that can create jobs—the world has changed, our solutions haven't, and the result has been a disaster, politically as well as otherwise!

It would be impossible to still have 8.3% unemployment if we were on the right path [the result is the proof]—and among other problems with this concept--if the market fails, the unemployed are out of luck [It is the reason Romeny's job creation solution is a farce!].

Further, unemployment is a "social" problem we are seeking to address with a highly unstable, incompatible entity: The Market -- That is, the last place we should look for a reliable solution to our unemployment crisis is The Market....

And, what apparently isn't clear going forward in the 21st Century, is that an expanding and contracting public workforce is an INDISPENSABLE component to the correct functioning of a modern market economy—i.e., The Humphrey-Hawkins Full Employment Act was dead-on correct in 1978—and provided a "win-win" solution for America--

The market thrives when we have a robust, employed, consuming workforce, and it is essential to consumer confidence—and overlooked is that HR 870 [currently in Committee], and the proposed "Neighbor-To-Neighbor Job Creation Act" [hereafter NTN] See: www.Inclusivism.org [both authorized under Humphrey-Hawkins], are deficit-neutral--Pro-Market "win-win" solutions: The American people win, and capitalism wins—

CHAPTER TWO

President Obama/Fellow Democrats:

For the past 65 years we have had two parallel paths to address unemployment in America—

To assure employment for the troops returning from WW II, President Truman signed into law The Full Employment Act of 1946—

This was expanded upon in 1978 with the Humphrey-Hawkins Full Employment Act, signed into law by President Carter—

And a 21st Century version of this path to full employment in America, is pending the House, HR 870.

Humphrey-Hawkins best defines this path to addressing unemployment in America, and it "authorizes" our government to create a "reservoir of public employees" anytime our unemployment rises above "3%".

And in spite of the fact that this path to employment has been the law of the land since 1946—and is a Pro-Market solution [more on this shortly]---Washington has lacked the wherewithal to implement this path to employment on behalf of the American people—[a point not lost on the "occupy" movement].

Rather, Washington has taken the alternate parallel path—by insisting that human labor is a "component" in the free enterprise system—[barely distinguishable from the machine the human operates] to be used and discarded "at will"—and the Republican propaganda is that it is an attack upon "freedom" to challenge this concept, but whose "freedom"?

As a result, however, "conventional wisdom" has insisted that it is the market, alone, that can fix our unemployment crisis—the result has been a disaster—

The market thrives when we have a robust, employed, consuming public—and by taking this parallel path—we not only have a staggering 8.1% unemployment, but a struggling recovery as well.

Ironically, following WW II, Australia passed a law very similar to our Full Employment Act of 1946—

Difference is—they actually put it into effect—and over the next 30 years—[until the cold winds of conservatism swept in Reagan and Thatcher, etc.] –the government in Australia saw as a solemn responsibility that "anyone willing to work should be provided with a job" [a quote from the "Audacity of Hope"].

The citizens of Australia still refer to this 30 years as their "Golden Age".

Jim Green, Democrat candidate for Congress, 2000 www.Inclusivism.org

CHAPTER THREE

NOTE: In response to Romney's 47% who need to "take responsibility for their lives"....

Editor/NYTimes:

What is most interesting about Romney saying our troops in Afghanistan are "freeloaders"—yes folks, our troops, who are exempt from paying income taxes, are part of that 47% Romney said are "freeloaders" who don't pay "income taxes"—and need to "take responsibility for their lives"--

But what is most interesting about Romney's divisive "entitlement" nonsense—that half the country are "moochers" is that by his definition--he is talking about almost every rank and file Republican he is asking to vote for him!

And we need to drill down on in this "mind-set"—exclusive to the Republican political strategy, today, which is riddled with lies and half-truths--it is what distinguishes them from Goldwater Republicans—

Folks, if your child has a lemonade stand—THEY PAY TAXES—[and are paying at a higher tax rate than Romney/Romeny propose for themselves]—that is, every person who participates in our economy pays taxes!

The half-truth in the "income tax" PORTION of our paying taxes—is that every working person pays payroll taxes, sales taxes, and most pay property taxes--and with home interest deduction, etc., that PORTION of their paying taxes is exempt!

And an ironic twist in this "freeloaders" nonsense who don't pay any "income tax"— we have 2000 millionaires who, through high paid tax attorneys, etc.—DON'T pay any "income tax"!

But by the Republicans using "income taxes"—this is interpreted by our ignorant and uninformed as "Oh my God, 47% of Americans are on the dole"—AND THAT IS EXACTLY WHAT ROMNEY [the Republicans strategy] WANTS THEM TO BELIEVE! It is a bald-faced lie!

In short, TO DIVIDE US AMERICANS INTO THE "GOOD GUYS VS THE BAD GUYS"— and everyone voting Republican needs to ask if they have become a victim of this obscene tactic?

And, that is the Republican strategy in a nutshell, folks, and they have been feverishly working to perfect it over the past 30 plus years—

We are a "victim" if we are voting against our own economic interests—and the economic interest of our children—

We are a "representative" government, folks—and Romney/Ryan "represents" the rich getting richer [and solely for their personal GREED], and us 99% getting poorer—PERIOD—THEY HAVE NO OTHER PROGRAM!

Finally, if their lips are moving—on FOX, or Limbaugh, etc., etc.,--it is to divide Americans into the "GOOD GUYS VS THE BAD GUYS"—rather than bringing America together in the best interest of Americans, and America!

Jim Green, Democrat candidate for Congress, 2000—See also: MY LETTERS TO PRESIDENT OBAMA, on Amazon/Kindle

CHAPTER FOUR

NOTE: The following is in response to a letter riddled with Republican talking points--in my local paper—it could apply to any city in America....[the names have been changed to protect the guilty]....

Letter to the editor:

Interesting letter from "C E" -- "An economic lesson" on September 9, 2012—I hope he's setting down for my response—

"C" went on a rant, i.e., lecturing about "profit" but fails to mention that more businesses have failed over the past 32 years—as a DIRECT result of Republican policies, and when the Republicans have been in the White House--than in any like period in American history!

Yes, "C"—it is Republican policies that are anti-capitalism—it is their policies that undermine our market economy—and it is long past due to set the record straight regarding the canard that the Republicans are the "pro-business" party—the facts do not support this, excuse the phrase-- "Big Lie"!

We cannot siphon America's wealth away from the consuming middle—and give it to the 1% in obscene tax cuts [GREED JUST FOR THE SAKE OF GREED—the Republican One and Only agenda]—without sending our economy into a tailspin!

And what a joke—attacking President Obama on "redistribution of wealth"—when this has been bedrock Republican policy since 1980 to redistribute America's wealth to the 1%--and we now have 400 persons who hold more of America's wealth than 150 million of the rest of us!

And as you will recall, "C", as did occur in 1987 [Reagan] and again in 2008 [Bush] – and the American taxpayers were forced to rush in with trillions of dollars to prevent another Great Depression!

Romeny said he would let GM go bankrupt [the Republican solution]—but I'm betting our local GM dealer [our auto industry all across America] will tell you that President Obama got it right!

Surely, "C", you will give credit to President Obama for saving this "for profit" business—and the jobs of a million Americans employed in this industry—won't you?

Actually, I'm glad "C" wrote this letter because it provides the opportunity to expose a whopper by the Republican Party: That "Greed just for the sake of greed [cut taxes for the 1%]" --and "being pro-business" are the same thing---

When IN FACT, they are as different as night and day!

For instance, if cutting taxes for the 1% created jobs [Romney's ONE AND ONLY JOB CREATION SOLUTION], but if this actually

worked we would have full employment—
BECAUSE THE BUSH TAX CUTS WERE
EXTENDED!

And Romney/Ryan wants to cut their taxes,
and drive up our deficit up even further—
and let's be honest, "C", they want to pick up
right where Bush II left off—and we all
know how that turned out!

This letter could turn into a book regarding
the inaccuracies about our economy in "C's"
letter—and in pointing out that if Ryan's lips
are moving, he's lying---but time doesn't
permit, and will have to saved for another
day.

In closing, "C", here is something to chew
on—these billionaires you celebrate and who

are trying to buy this election---made their billions off of us—the American people—so why do they hide this money in the Cayman Islands, and Swiss bank accounts—to avoid paying taxes and purely for GREED—rather than investing in the betterment of America? Where is their fiduciary obligation to the American people—who made them rich?

Jim Green

CHAPTER FIVE

Memo to Economic Policy Institute:

In my experience, the "consciousness level" for persons regarding rights for the American "employee", in the work place— are all over the map---with some persons being acutely aware of the necessity for employees having rights, and also what those rights might be-----

To others who are oblivious—i.e., draw a blank regarding this subject—and thus chase down blind alleys in looking for solutions to the urgent "social" problem of ubiquitous unemployment—and are blinded to any solution that is not "market" driven [the worst place to look for a viable solution]....

And which almost always start with the fallacy is in believing that we can not fix "unemployment" and the "economy" at the same time—when the correct answer is –of course we can—

But when we are stuck in the mind-set that it is only the "market" that can create jobs— we close our mind to alternative solutions— i.e., alternative solutions are not even on the table—even on the Radar—they are invisible to our "problem solvers"—who, sadly [and perhaps a slight exaggeration], still have one foot on the plantation—

And the myth that "public sector" jobs undermines the "pool of slaves" [the unspoken mind-set] from which "private jobs" are derived, and to be used and discarded "at will" [our current "conventional wisdom"]--

And the proof: For the above to be untrue—HR 870, currently pending in Committee in the House—and which could reduce our unemployment to "3%" within a year of passage—would be front and center—a top priority for our "problem solvers"---

When, in fact, most never even heard of this proposed law—let alone, the public—and there is a blind spot to a major flaw in the "market only" job creation solution: If the market fails, the unemployed are out of luck—

In short, the "market only" approach gives lip service to solving our unemployment crisis—[rather than looking at it as a "stand alone" social problem—independent of he market]—i.e., it is seen as and a step-child in the process—and 8% unemployment is the result—

Jim Green, Democrat candidate for Congress, 2000

CHAPTER SIX

NOTE: Until we fix our Electronic Voting Machine nightmare—we have little hope in effective change.

So long as the potential for manipulation of electronic voting continues to exist—our elections in America will be in peril! In spite of all the polls showing a strong Obama victory--it was not until 10PM Central on 11-4-08.....that we could breath a sigh of relief....we had been cheated out of the past two elections....with many believing that Bush was never legally elected president of the United States....and we were braced for the worst.......this can, and MUST be fixed before 2012, so that this never happens again, and in the interest of all who support fair and open elections--regardless of party. Accordingly, it is urged that we adopt the following proposed "FAIL-SAFE ELECTRONIC VOTING ACT":

THE FAIL-SAFE ELECTRONIC VOTING ACT

1) EVERY electronic voting machine (hereafter EVM), must be inexpensive, identical throughout the U.S. in a 1/150 ratio, and *must count and produce a hard-copy of the recorded votes.* In addition, an extra copy of their recorded votes would be produced (not necessarily a hard-copy), marked "Voter's Copy", and containing "NOTICE: Do Not Destroy Until Every Election On Your Ballot Is Certified". [If Wal-Mart refused to give us a receipt for our purchases—would they not be suspect—and

this regards our democracy].

2) *After confirming that their votes are recorded correctly,* the voter would then insert the hard-copy ballot into a software-free (count only) optical scanner (hereafter OS), for a second count. The hard-copy ballot would be retained by election officials in the event a candidate asks for a recount (*not possible under the current system, and which undermines the legality of each such election).* The EVM and the OS must be manufactured by different companies (which is universally true today).

3) Election officials assigned to oversee the EVM, would be prevented by law from overseeing the OS, and vice-versa, and stiff

criminal penalties would be imposed for violations.

4) Further, every EVM would be programmed with raw data re the total registration rolls, by party, and norms for their voting history, etc.,----as an "alert" to a possible irregularity, such as an "Under-vote"—or "vote-flipping" etc., and _standards_ established to suspend certification where there is an "improbable result", at least temporarily, of a particular election until the discrepancy is cleared up. (This is what computers do best, and it would be very easy to create such a program).

5) At the end of the election day, tallies would be taken from the EVM and the OS, for each candidate. _If the tallies didn't_

balance for any given election, or if there is
an "alert", that election cannot be certified
until the "error" is corrected If the
candidates agree (the victory is certain),
minor discrepancies in the count could be
disregarded. While probably rare, the Voter,
or a random sample of Voters, would be
required by law to return their Copy of the
recorded votes to the election office to clear
up any "error", or where an "alert" signals the
need for same.

6) Further, every state provides for a recount
when the total vote falls below a certain
percent of difference between the
candidates, impossible to conduct with the
current EVM—and thus Congress must
mandate the following regarding
presidential candidates: A RUN–OFF election

is mandated and triggered in those states where the percent of total vote is less than .5% of difference between any given candidates; said election to be held on the second Saturday following the election, on PAPER BALLOTS ONLY, and contain ONLY the names of the relevant candidates, for instance: "Barack Obama, Democrat" and "John McCain, Republican"—with oversight in counting by a representative(s) of each party—said procedure providing more than adequate time to meet the Electoral College mandate. NOTE: Had this been the law in 2000, Al Gore would be our president, and the American economy would not be in meltdown!

7) Finally, absent the above safeguards, and until these safeguards are in place--

Congress must mandate that PAPER BALLOTS, ONLY, can be used in our presidential elections. This is not a "partisan" issue, it is a "pro-democracy" issue. Most importantly, this will return the responsibility for our elections, and our vote counting, back into the hands of the individual voter, where it belongs, and out of the hands of "corporate control"--- *it is after all "our democracy", itself, that is at risk if we don't take these steps---and in that regard, is there any time or cost differential that is too great?*

Reply To: Jim Green -- Democrat candidate for Congress, Dist 21, TX, 2000
jgreen5@satx.rr.com
www.Inclusivism.org

CHAPTER SEVEN

Editor/NY Times:

The Republican strategy in this election--the same as with President Truman in 1948--is to speak of President Obama as if he is a person who doesn't know how to tie his own shoes—hmmmm…

For the 18% who will not vote for Romney because he is Mormon, the 16% of women who favor President Obama over Romney/Ryan—and 0% of blacks who will vote for R/R—this strategy is obviously not working—

Integral to this strategy, however, is a wanton disregard for FACTS [by their own statement], and the TRUTH—indeed, possibly the most egregious in American history—but consistent with the Republican strategy to lie, cheat and rob to get elected—so they can again lie, cheat and rob America blind, if elected!

But we need to drill down on that faction in America, many closet racists, who are indifferent to this specious Republican strategy—and to whom this strategy is directed—

For instance, yesterday, at the doctor's office, I engaged a fellow senior about the election [us older, white guys all have an opinion— on everything]—

But he wanted to give me $5 to go see the "birther" movie "2016" [apparently believing that I needed to be "informed"]—and when I informed him that this was a propaganda film [the same strategy Hitler used]—and that it was riddled with lies [and totally disregards, or is ignorant of the fact that "Hawaii is a STATE"]—

He told me that he didn't care "if the movie is riddled with LIES"!

Whoa, folks—this is new, and it is dangerous--we are into a whole new gear, here, folks, and perhaps this is what distinguishes this from every previous election in American history!

A democracy will only work by our having an "informed" electorate—we cannot make accurate decisions—without accurate facts--

but when we have a faction of our electorate who don't care if Romney and Ryan are lying [if Ryan's lips are moving....]—or that propaganda put out by the Republican Party is false----this means America is headed for a world of hurt—picture this—if the engineers lied regarding the data in our moon landing would we Americans have accomplished this amazing feat?

The odds makers give President Obama a 75% chance of winning—but with the fraudulent "vote fraud" legislation in our battleground states, and the manipulation of our flawed electronic voting system—and President Obama is cheated out of this election—

It is US, the American people, and an America based on a foundation of fraud and lies—that will be forced to suffer the consequences! HINT: If you don't care if R/R are liars—Do AMERICA a favor and DON'T VOTE!

Jim Green, Democrat candidate for Congress, 2000 [See also: "Why President Obama Lost The 2012 Election" on Amazon/Kindle]

CHAPTER EIGHT

Editor/NYTimes:

There is a wise and trusted adage "Don't change horses in the middle of the stream" and never has it had more relevance than in this election—

As we are all aware, except for those who are comatose—our economy was in a major meltdown when President Obama took office—we were losing 700,000 jobs a month—and 2.8 million jobs had already been lost in 2008—with the rate of loss matched only with the Great Depression--

The situation demanded action—NOW!

The lesson from the Great Depression has an interesting medical metaphor—and ironically, we discovered our error somewhat in the same time-frame. Prior to the 30's conventional medical wisdom held that the way to treat "shock" was by cutting off the blood supply—and not infrequently the patient died—

In response to the collapse of the market in 1929, it was the conclusion of the FED to cut off the money supply—which, as we all know now, drove the economy straight over a cliff—and prolonged the Depression by at least 10 years!

The lesson learned in medicine in the treatment of "shock" was to increase the blood supply, not cut it—and for our economy, every credible economist since agree that to fix our economy we need to infuse it with cash—and plenty of it!

Fast forward to today: It is interesting the selective memory loss on the part of Republicans regarding our "Stimulus Bill"—No, not the one by President Obama—but rather the one by President Bush on February 8, 2008 [where was the Tea Party, then?]—when the storm clouds posed an ominous economic future—and then the $700 billion TARP signed by President Bush, later in 2008—

But when President Obama's Stimulus Bill came along in February, 2009 [on the advice of every credible economist in America, on the right or left]—and a third in tax cuts—

the Republican propaganda machine went into high gear to paint him as a "tax and spend" liberal—The lying SOB's—And the lie continues to this day!

Jim Green, Democrat candidate for Congress, 2000

CHAPTER NINE

EDITOR/NYTimes:

RE DEBATES: WHERE IS THE ROMNEY APOLOGY?

James Baker, former Treasury Secretary under President Reagan, wildly praised President Obama on Fareed Zakaria's GPS, in early 2009—for using the "Stimulus" to put a floor under our economy in meltdown—

The reason: Because Baker did the EXACT same thing in 1987—following Black Monday, October 19, 1987—when the Market lost a quarter of its value in one day and our economic experts were predicting another Great Depression…

So where was the Tea Party then—blathering on about Reagan/Baker being "tax and spend" liberals? —[The Romney/Ryan "cheap shot" being taken at President Obama—and devoid of decency]—And to this day virtually every "rank and file" Republican believes that President Obama is a wild "tax and spend" liberal—as a result of the "Stimulus"— Absent an APOLOGY!

It is obvious that President Obama would have vastly preferred spending the $6 trillion making America energy independent and on developing alternative fuel sources—

But as both Treasury Secretaries, Baker and Geithner, fully understood—the "Stimulus" was the lesson from the Great Depression—

when the FED erroneously cut off the money supply, then, and prolonged the Great Depression by 10 years!

The "Stimulus" was the ONLY doctor in Town—and what has not been said by anyone—if McCain had won he would have spent the same $6 trillion [maybe more]—because that would have been the advice of every credible economist in America—on the right or left!

The fact is, Reaganomics—which Romney promises to return to, if elected—has a shelf-life of 7 years before the economy collapses under the weight of the false premise upon which it is based!

We cannot siphon America's wealth away from the consuming middle and add the short-fall in revenue created by obscene tax cuts to the 1%, to the deficit [Reaganomics by definition]—without driving our deficit through the overheads, exploding our unemployment, and driving our economy over a cliff!

Our deficit was only $60 billion, in 1980—as a result of inept and corrupt Reaganomics—the Republicans ran our deficit to a criminal $10 trillion by 2008—and the above was the result!

And Romney should not be permitted to say another word in this election, or in the Presidential Debates—until he profusely apologizes to the American people for the

DAMAGE Republican policies did to America—as a matter of DECENCY!

Jim Green, Democrat candidate for Congress, 2000 [See also: "My Letters To President Obama" on Amazon/Kindle]

CHAPTER TEN

MEMO: Economic Policy Institute

The missing component in our job creation solutions is "the human need to work and be a productive human being"—and evident in the statement that "anybody willing to work should be able to find a job".

Had this been factored into our "mind-set" about how to fix our unemployment crisis— our approach, and the outcome, would have been totally different.

Unfortunately, however, Republicans and Democrats—[our conventional 'wisdom'] is still laboring under the myth, advocated by conservatives, that "humans are lazy and don't want to work"—and evident by our celebrating "Welfare-To-Work" [to get those lazy bums off the dole]—an egregious insult to human integrity, and to the true nature of man!

In short, we should be holding our head in shame regarding this ugly insult—most on welfare would have much preferred to have been working all along, but people cannot apply for jobs that don't exist—[the point most missed—and needed to be fixed]--and we are now paying the price—THAT WE GOT IT WRONG—failed to factor in "the human need to work and be a productive human being"— !

And, Our 8.1% unemployment rate is consummate proof—

Jim Green, Democrat candidate for Congress, 2000

CHAPTER ELEVEN

POSTED ON FACEBOOK:

The FRAUD in the bogus voter ID laws invented by radical Republicans at ALEC— are the laws themselves—i.e., where is our federal law making it illegal to perpetrate this FRAUD on the American people to suppress the vote—in violation of the Voting Rights Act--with fines/imprisonment for anyone perpetuating this FRAUD? Jim Green, Democrat candidate for Congress, 2000

CHAPTER TWELVE

President Obama/Fellow Democrats:

Kansas is my home state [currently live in Texas]—hometown El Dorado--

Following the 2010 election, the Republican-controlled Kansas legislature passed a voter ID law [part of the behind closed door scam perpetrated on the American people by ALEC—and cropping up in Republican-controlled statehouses all across America since the 2010 election—albeit, not news to the informed].

The following is a personal experience with this law—and the criminal suppression of the vote--

In a conversation with my older brother [a retired attorney], yesterday—and a life-long Democrat—he was told that he would need a new photo for his ID—which could only be taken with a particular camera—but when he asked to have his picture taken—was told the camera was broken!

My brother is 88, he was a former U.S. Attorney under President Kennedy!

If he is prevented from voting—how far reaching can this criminal suppression of the vote extend?

Our democracy is under siege on two fronts in this election, fellow Democrats—and we need to create federal legislation making both illegal—declaring them to be unconstitutional—[and while having zero chance of passing the House—the legislation would create public awareness and act as a warning to the electorate].

1] Declare Citizens United to be unconstitutional [it put America up for sale to the highest bidder] and reinstate contribution restrictions to a pre-Citizens United status [or better, mandate public financing of our elections].

2] Make it unlawful to suppress the vote with the fraudulent claim of "voter fraud"— when there is virtually no evidence of same—and make it a crime punishable by fine/imprisonment to suppress the vote by perpetuating this fraud. In the balancing of interests—the right to vote is infinitely greater.

Finally, it would also be ideal if we could limit the Republicans to not more than one lie on any given day—in their "Big Lie" strategy to steal the presidency—except that Ryan would be arrested before breakfast—

But levity aside, fellow Democrats, we have a crisis on our hands—and while the above may not be acceptable—we have a constitutional imperative on our hands and we can't stand idly by and just let it happen….IMHO

Jim Green, Democrat candidate for Congress, 2000 –See also: "OUR GREED &

IGNORANCE: Poses A Far Greater Threat To America, Than Terrorism" on Amazon/Kindle

CHAPTER FOURTEEN

Editor/NYTimes:

For the better part of the past 20 years I have corresponded with a professor at Rutgers University—and a few years back we got into a protracted discussion regarding the definition of "self-esteem".

I don't think we can overestimate the relevance and impact of this concept on our elections.

The discussion started when a study " The Dark Side of High Self-Esteem" reported that criminals have "high self-esteem".

I've seen a few flawed studies—but this took the cake—i.e., the premise is patently absurd—and the "researchers" had confused "high self-esteem" with "arrogance"—I argued, and this is where the discussion started—

To drill down abit—I asked if Hitler was a person with "high self-esteem"—his answer is at the conclusion—

Our discussion explored two opposing points of view—one, "internal"—the other "external". The "internal" is based on an internal sense of one's own sense of self-worth—irrelevant to external factors [the definition of high self-esteem I adhere to].

While "external" regards a person basing their "self-esteem"—their self worth on props they surround themselves with—such as a house, or car—or on a more personal level—their looks, or a good head of hair.

Problem is, given the vagaries of life we can lose our external props—and we get old-- and can lose our hair.

With the lesson being that creating our sense of self worth on the latter…on external factors, is ephemeral—not an accurate measure of, or a correct definition of "high self-esteem".

The over-arching point of this discourse is the belief [and I am certain that I am correct, on this] that we have an epidemic of "low self-esteem" in America—our angry, old white guys who vote Republican—as an external prop to bolster their feelings of low self-esteem—to make themselves feel important—and it is destroying America!

Data shows that 50% of these pathetic souls have the delusion that they will be millionaires someday—and they vote Republican—so they will be prepared—even though they may not have a pot to piss in— and are voting against the economic interests of their children! It is the premise of "What's The Matter With Kansas"

We cannot over-estimate the danger these loonies pose to America—

Jim Green, Democrat candidate for Congress, 2000

CHAPTER FIFTEEN

Editor/NYTimes:

Folks---We need to pull back the curtain and look at what is really behind the Republican agenda in this election:

First, we have tiny, tiny, tiny handful of Americans who are willing to chip in over a billion dollars to get Romney/Ryan elected—

And we need to drill down on who these folks are, and ask what do they want? For one, these are business people—they are not going to gamble that kind of cash unless they plan on getting a payoff for their gamble—

And their payoff, folks, is to have their taxes cut even further—so they can turn their billion dollars, into two billion—and not just via the tax cuts but also by hiding their cash in tax sheltered accounts in the Cayman Islands, etc., rather than investing in America, ad nauseam!

In short, folks—if this tiny, tiny, tiny handful [the 1%] is chipping in over a billion dollars to get Romney/Ryan elected--the last candidates us 99% should be voting for—is Romney/Ryan!

Jim Green, Democrat candidate for Congress, 2000

CHAPTER SIXTEEN

Editor/NY Times

There will be a lot of "buyer's remorse" on the part of rank and file Republicans—who voted for Romney/Ryan—if they should actually win—

They will be like the guy who woke up from a serious hangover and found out he had thrown the family cat through the neighbor's window [an old Shelley Berman joke]—

Most of the rank and file I have talked to are so blindly zealous in their vote "against" President Obama—[some based on racism]--they don't have a clue what Romney/Ryan has in store for them.

Specifically, to pick up right where Bush II left off—and we all know how that turned out! Been there—did that—it is called "Supply-Side" or "Reaganomics"—IT DOESN'T WORK! IT IS WHAT CAUSED THE GREAT RECESSION IN 2008!

The national Republican Party has but a single agenda—TO PANDER TO THE GREED OF THEIR WEALTHIEST CONTRIBUTORS! Period! That's it—and rather than investing in the betterment of America, they hide their wealth in secret bank accounts to avoid investing in America--!

Further, we can't siphon America's wealth away from the consuming middle, and give it to the already wealthy, without sending our economy into a tailspin!

"Supply-Side" has a shelf-life of about 7 years before the false premise upon which it is based starts caving in on itself—as we learned in our economic collapse in 1987 and again in 2008 [and getting worse each salvo from this corrupt scheme]—and it has cost the American taxpayers trillions of dollars to put a floor under our economy, in the inevitable meltdown!

President Obama had the grim task, from his first day in office, of saving America from another Great Depression, in 2009—

And the Republican propaganda machine has the gall to snow the rank and file with the false blather [flat out lie] that Obama was a "tax and spend" liberal—Obama is a moderate CONSERVATIVE! And if McCain had been elected he would have taken the exact same steps—the choice was "Stimulus" or an ultra-severe Depression—Period! We were losing 700,000 jobs a month!

Finally, the starting point in our political discussion in this election—MUST begin with a Republican apology as assurance to the American people they will not return to the same failed policies that almost sunk America!

So what rank and file Republicans should be asking, now, is where is the Romney/Ryan profuse apology to the American people for the damage Republican policies have done to America?

Jim Green, Democrat candidate for Congress, 2000 See also: My Letters To President Obama, on Amazon/Kindle

CHAPTER SEVENTEEN

Letter to editor/NY Times:

Doesn't it strike anyone as odd that Paul Ryan rails, daily, over deficits under President Obama—indeed, holding himself out, now, as a champion of deficit reduction—WHEN he voted to drive up our deficit by over $5 trillion, while in Congress, under Bush II!

Actually, "odd" may be too kind—maybe "disingenuous" [which is the polite way to say someone is a lying SOB]—"Aw shucks", Ryan is a lying hypocrite—it is the only honest description that fits!

And to add insult to injury, Ryan now wants to decimate [i.e., destroy] Medicare—[read Ryan's Budget]--so he can give the money saved to the Republican's wealthiest contributors—their payoff for getting him elected! What a guy!

We won't even go to his Draconian approach regarding "women's rights", [including being anti-choice]—and evident by his co-sponsoring legislation with Akin, Ad Nauseam!

And he is doing all of this while claiming to be a "Christian" [actually Catholic]—seems he has forgotten that if one is not following the teachings of Christ, one is NOT a Christian! Which the "Nuns On A Bus" have been quick to remind him!

And if the reader does not know that the sole agenda of the National Republican Party, the same as Ryan, is to make the rich, richer— and them poorer—they are not paying attention!

But getting back to the deficit, please consider this metaphor: If one of our children spills a glass of milk—we wipe it up with some paper towels—but if they spill a whole gallon—we grab a mop and a bucket and everything else at hand to clean up the mess—

And, President Obama was handed a mega-spill to clean up—from day one—as a direct result of the mess caused by Ryan, and the rest of the Republicans over the past 8 years!

In short, it cost us—the American taxpayers $4 trillion just to clean up the $10 trillion mess left by the Republicans, i.e., it was this "mop and bucket" President Obama had to use to prevent another Great Depression!

Finally, you would think Romney and company would, first, profusely apologize to the American people for the mess they left— and then promise never to pull this gimmick on the American people again--

But they have the gall to tell us they are going to double-down—i.e., pick up right where Bush II left off!

Do they think we are stupid? Don't answer that….

Jim Green, Democrat candidate for Congress, 2000 [See also: "My Letters To President Obama", and "Why President Obama Lost The 2012 Election: A wake-up call", on Amazon/Kindle

CHAPTER EIGHTEEN

Editor/NY Times:

A Republican candidate for president said "On next January 20, there will begin in Washington, the biggest unraveling, unsnarling, untangling operation in our nation's history."

But before Republican ideologues say "right on" regarding President Obama—this was from an archive speech by Republican candidate Tom Dewey, and directed at President Truman, in 1948.

Will politics never change? Given the political rhetoric you would think President Truman couldn't even tie his own shoes—

albeit, he had ended WWII [while President Obama has rescued America from another Great Depression].

And other parallels between these two elections are even more striking.

For instance, Truman was outraged by what he called a "Do nothing Congress"—and he went on the warn the electorate that "The country cannot afford another Republican Congress." Are we in an echo chamber, here?

The most startling parallel, however, is when Truman said of the Republican Congress on a stump speech "It is a sad tale of the sell out of the American people to these gluttons of privilege—these cold men who skim the cream from our natural resources to satisfy their own greed."

This could have been said yesterday, and yet, it was said by President Truman 64 years ago!

Finally, President Truman offered some words of wisdom to the American electorate on the danger or returning our government back to the Republicans [as true today, as then] "I'm just waking you up to the fact that this is YOUR fight—and YOU are going to be the loser [if you return the White House back to the Republicans]."

And, as every student of History knows, and in spite of the inexcusable headline error by

the Chicago Tribune "DEWEY DEFEATS
TRUMAN"—President Truman won.

Jim Green, Democrat candidate for Congress,
2000

CHAPTER NINETEEN

I can't resist including the following—our problem solving is stifled in all kinds of subtle ways as a result of the following…and yes, I plead guilty—I am the author….

A MESSAGE FROM GOD

MANY CENTURIES AGO, a man of the cloth, we don't know his name, and in a flash of insight (perhaps induced by peyote) told his flock that "sex is a sin". And lo and behold he learned that by taking a very natural and healthy part of our life and turning it into something that was "dirty and nasty", that he could imprison his flock, and fill his coffers, and hallelujah it was a great day for the Lord!

Quickly, his miracle spread to other churches in his village, and then to the next village, and then the next county and then state and then it spread to all the churches in the ancient world, and all of their flocks cowed in fear and shame and became imprisoned, and their coffers over-floweth. Hallelujah, it was a great day for the Lord!

And to keep the myth alive they started inventing stories, half-baked stories, that made no sense to anyone who is rational, such as "Mary was a virgin"—well, she just had to be a virgin because she would never partake in anything that was dirty and nasty, like sex (if you're doing it right), and this was necessary to make "sex is a sin" make sense...so they invented a Mary that was "sinless"--you get the picture. And it is apparent that God had to make sex very pleasurable just to overcome all the bullshit. And their coffers over-floweth. Hallelujah, it was a great day for the Lord!

No one seemed to be bothered that when we play tricks on the human mind by taking something that is very natural and healthy, such as sex, and make it dirty and nasty that all kinds of bad things happen to the human mind.

Such as most pedophiles, and most serial killers, and voting Republican, and unwarranted suicides, and most mental illness, and unwanted pregnancies. (Teens not wanting to have sex is the perversion, not the other way around, and by replacing sex education and condoms, with unrealistic "abstinence", and by using blather about "low self-esteem" to shame them into not "sinning"--We have a teen pregnancy in the U.S. twice that of England and Canada!).

But none of this mattered, because their coffers over-floweth, and Hallelujah, it is a great day for the Lord!

There is a cure--------Tell these right-wing loonies to shove it....

GOD

ABOUT THE AUTHOR. I was employed in our

Criminal Justice System for a cumulative 20 years

as a probation officer, with 5 of those years as a

chief probation officer. I authored the concept of

"Shock Incarceration" which became law in Kansas in 1970, and then was adopted in numerous jurisdictions in the U.S. and also spread to Europe—it is currently identified in the U.S. as

"Boot Camp" [as the means to "shock" the young
offender—and a total distortion of my original
intent—like many ideas, once released, they take
on a life of their own and I have also seen
referred to as "Scared Straight" and "A taste
of prison"]. I was the Democrat candidate
for Congress, District 21, TX, 2000. I
would most define myself as a Social
Ecologist--
[albeit my degree is in Psychology]. My web
page
is www.Inclusivism.org –which has been on
the
internet since 1996.

Other books by the author on
Amazon/Kindle:

MY LETTERS TO PRESIDENT OBAMA,
LETTERS ON STEROIDS, THE HARVARD
BOYS CLUB [my first], WHY PRESIDENT
OBAMA LOST THE 2012 ELECTION: A
Wake-Up Call [for our amnesic], and THE
FIRST TIME I HAD SEX [a response to our
oppressive radical religious right], OUR
GREED AND IGNORANCE: Poses A Far
Greater Threat To America, Than Terrorism